A COMPLETE INTRODUCTION TO

BUDGERIGARS

Some of the different budgerigar color varieties.

A COMPLETE INTRODUCTION TO
BUDGERIGARS

COMPLETELY ILLUSTRATED IN FULL COLOR

Three young Dominant Pied budgerigars with their father.

Tony David

Budgerigars offer a wide range of different colors from which to choose—but regardless of color, they're all enjoyable pets.

Photographs: L. Arnall, 81, 83 top, 87 bottom, 88, 90, 91. Archiv Klinik für Geflügel TiHo Hannover, 86. Dr. Herbert R. Axelrod, 36, 49, 68. Penny Corbett & Stephanie Logue, 43. Kerry V. Donnelly, 73. Leonard J. Eisenberg, 75 top. Michael Gilroy, 5, 38, 52, 70, 76, 77. Ray Hanson, 20. Fred Harris, 30 bottom. M. Heidenreich, 80, 87 top. N. Kummerfeld, 79, 85 top. Harry V. Lacey, 7, 40, 50, 60, 62, 63, 75 bottom, 78, 83 bottom, 84, 85. bottom. Aaron Norman, 65. Courtesy of San Diego Zoo, 46. Vincent Serbin, 37. Tony Silva, 19. Louise Van der Meid, 20, 22, 26, 28, 30 top, 32, 33 top, 34 bottom, 48, 82, 94–95. Wayne Wallace, 10, 15, 33 bottom, 34 top, 44, 69.

Distributed in the UNITED STATES by T.F.H. Publications, Inc., 211 West Sylvania Avenue, Neptune City, NJ 07753; in CANADA to the Pet Trade by H & L Pet Supplies Inc., 27 Kingston Crescent, Kitchener, Ontario N2B 2T6; Rolf C. Hagen Ltd., 3225 Sartelon Street, Montreal 382 Quebec; in CANADA to the Book Trade by Macmillan of Canada (A Division of Canada Publishing Corporation), 164 Commander Boulevard, Agincourt, Ontario M1S 3C7; in ENGLAND by T.F.H. Publications Limited, 4 Kier Park, Ascot, Berkshire SL5 7DS; in AUSTRALIA AND THE SOUTH PACIFIC by T.F.H. (Australia) Pty. Ltd., Box 149, Brookvale 2100 N.S.W., Australia; in NEW ZEALAND by Ross Haines & Son, Ltd., 18 Monmouth Street, Grey Lynn, Auckland 2 New Zealand; in SINGAPORE AND MALAYSIA by MPH Distributors (S) Pte., Ltd., 601 Sims Drive, #03/07/21, Singapore 1438; in the PHILIPPINES by Bio-Research, 5 Lippay Street, San Lorenzo Village, Makati Rizal; in SOUTH AFRICA by Multipet Pty. Ltd., 30 Turners Avenue, Durban 4001. Published by T.F.H. Publications Inc. Manufactured in the United States of America by T.F.H. Publications, Inc.

Contents

Budgerigars—Their Past and Present

During his exploration of the arid interior of Australia, the nineteenth century ornithologist John Gould encountered a species of parakeet which had been first described in 1794. When he returned to Britain in 1840, he brought a pair of these parakeets with him, and they were the first living examples seen outside Australia, although a stuffed specimen had been in the possession of the London Linnean Society since 1831. Their name was corrupted from the Aboriginal term 'Betcherrygah', meaning 'good food', and so the birds became known as budgerigars.

The patterning of the budgerigar's wing coverts suggests undulating, or wavy, lines.

Other names, including Shell Parakeet and Undulated Grass Parakeet, have been used to describe these birds, which appear to have no close relations, apart from perhaps the *Neophema* parakeets, which also occur exclusively in Australia. The budgerigar's scientific name *Melopsittacus undulatus* is composed of the Greek words *melos* and *psittakos*, meaning 'song parrot' while the Latin *undulatus* translates as 'wavy-lined' and refers to the markings on the back and wings.

The appearance of mutations Yellows were soon reported in flocks of normal, or Light Green, budgerigars, and the skins of the Dark Green birds confirmed that color variations were not unknown in the wild. These parakeets are nomadic, wandering in search of the rains which stimulate the growth of the grasses on which they feed.

Gould's brother-in-law, Charles Coxen, was the first person to breed budgerigars in Europe and subsequently their popularity grew very rapidly. By the 1880's, when fewer birds were being imported from Australia to meet the demand, huge breeding establishments were set up on the continent. The Etablissement Bastide in France had up to 100,000 birds at any time, and such breeding units helped to establish some of the mutations which were appearing at this time.

MUTATIONS: Mutations from Light Greens

Yellow budgerigars occurred spontaneously in Belgium, being bred in 1872 from a pair of Light Greens. These birds, with their black eyes and mauve cheek patches, can be separated from Lutinos, which are a red-eyed variety. Although Lutinos first appeared in Belgium in 1879 and were bred in Britain five years later, this mutation was soon lost, until in 1936 it reappeared in Germany. On this occasion, Albino budgerigars, which became known during 1931, were used to recreate the Lutino mutation.

A fundamental change occurred in the Light Green budgerigar when a dark factor appeared in 1915, resulting in Dark Greens and leading to the production of Olive Greens, with two dark factors. These were also introduced to blue-series budgerigars, with Cobalts being bred in 1920, followed by Mauves. Visual Violets, which are currently one of the most sought-after colors, originated in 1936, and result from the combination of blue and dark factors, together with the violet, which is dominant and can be present as a single or double factor. The term 'Violet' can be applied to other colors, such as Light Green, and when it occurs in these birds, their color is darkened. 'Violet' is not therefore a color in itself, but exerts a modifying effect on other colors.

Pied budgerigars There are only two varieties of Pied budgerigars currently in existence, as the Dutch form appears to have been lost. The Australian Dominant Pied occurred in Sydney, Australia about 1935, and examples of this type then reached Europe during 1956 and also the United States. These early Pieds had yellow or white bands extending around their bodies, in conjunction with green- or blue-series markings, respectively. Between 1933 and 1934, just before the Dominant form appeared, Danish breeders, especially C. af Enehjelm, were instrumental in establishing strains of a recessive variety. These attractive budgerigars are still somewhat smaller than Dominant Pieds, and can be distinguished by their eyes, which lack the irides, appearing reddish in a good light.

Other colors In conjunction with the wide range of colors which can now be bred, it is also possible to superimpose other changes, often revolving around the black markings on the head, back and wings. Cinnamons for example, which originated in 1931, have brown markings instead of black, whereas these are grayish in the case of a Greywing. Yellow-wing and White-wing budgerigars, also known as Clearwings, are popular. These contribute to the parentage of 'Rainbows', which are strictly Yellow-faced Opaline White-wings. The retention of the yellow face in blue-series birds aroused considerable interest when it first occurred in Britain during 1935, and now a range of these attractive budgerigars is available. Good-quality Opalines should show a clear 'V' at the top of their wings and have lighter head markings

than normal.

So many possible color combinations have now been developed that it is impossible in a book of this size to cover them in any detail, but further information can be sought in other T.F.H. titles. Most breeders, after a general introduction to the hobby, start to specialize in a particular variety for exhibition purposes, at which time a basic understanding of the genetics of the chosen color or colors will prove of great value.

Feather mutations
Mutations affecting the feathering of budgerigars,

A flock of wild budgerigars coming to drink at a water hole in Australia.

as distinct from their coloration, have also been recorded. Long-flighted birds, whose flight feathers actually crossed, did not prove popular, but Crested Budgerigars are now becoming more common. This mutation occurred in several parts of the world, initially in Australia, then Canada and France, from 1935 onward. There are tufted, halfcircular and circular varieties, of which the latter, with a crest resembling that of a Gloster Corona canary, is most in demand. Many of these varieties have specialist clubs catering to those who keep particular mutations, and contact with breeders can be made through such channels. Advertisements in the bird-keeping magazines also give details both of available stock and club meetings, as well as containing information and articles contributed by many leading breeders.

New mutations In recent years, the number of new mutations reported has been relatively small. The Lacewing appeared in Britain during 1948, while

Skeletal anatomy of a budgerigar: the bones associated with the limbs are colored blue.

Clearbody budgerigars became established in the United States during the 1960's. It was with some excitement, therefore, that the Spangled mutation was reported from Australia in 1978. This is a dominant mutation, which leaves the body color unaltered. The feathering on the head and wings is edged with black, while the remainder of each feather is lighter, being the reverse of the normal pattern. It is similar in appearance to the Pearl form of the Cockatiel *(Nymphicus hollandicus),* and, furthermore, the spangled markings tend to be lost as the bird gets older. Spangled budgerigars are becoming more widely available, and other mutations, perhaps even a black budgerigar, will emerge in the future.

PURCHASING BUDGERIGARS:
Selecting healthy specimens

The condition of the feathering is of great importance when purchasing budgerigars. The birds must possess a full set of flight and tail feathers. Young budgerigars will lose some or all of these, the ends of the shafts containing dried blood, if they are suffering from french molt. This may be an inherited condition, or result from an infection of some kind, while nutritional factors have also been implicated. Those birds affected are known as 'runners', and in severe cases, remain handicapped for life.

The feathers around the vent, and also on the head must be clean and not stained or matted in any way. It does not matter, however, if spikes are seen among normal feathering, as this is a sign that the bird is molting. The new feathers emerge in sheaths, and unfurl as the outer waxy covering is removed, generally by preening. A budgerigar which appears to have its feathers fluffed up is probably ill, particularly if its eyes are closed. Finally, before choosing a budgerigar, its beak should be examined, to check that it is neither overgrown nor undershot.

For those interested in exhibiting their stock, the budgerigars should be obtained from a successful exhibitor, to lay the foundations of a good stud. Most breeders are pleased to assist newcomers to the Fancy, not only with stock but also with advice.

Clear eyes and sleek feathering indicate that a young budgerigar is healthy.

Aviaries and Birdrooms

The type of accommodation required will depend largely on the breeding system which is to be used. A basic aviary will suffice if the budgerigars are being bred on the colony system in the flight itself; otherwise extra space will be necessary for breeding cages. The first step is to find out what zoning ordinances may restrict the construction of an aviary, and local government offices will be able to advise on this matter.

AVIARIES

It is possible to purchase aviaries complete, in kit form for subsequent assembly, or to choose a design using a variety of wired panels. This latter method is often more convenient and makes for a more flexible system which may be expanded later without difficulty. Sectional structures only should be considered, as these can generally be moved quite easily, and re-erected elsewhere as required.

Construction of the aviary flight Building an outside flight for bugerigars is relatively easy to accomplish using timber 3.75 cm (1½ in) square for the framework, and 19G wire on the flight. It is convenient to construct the panels to the width of the wire which is to be used to cover them.

The typical aviary consists of a "flight" enclosed by wire which communicates with a solidly walled shelter via a flap door.

Units of 90 cm (3 ft) are often recommended therefore, although 120 cm (4 ft) and 180 cm (6 ft) widths of aviary mesh can also be obtained. Square or rectangular wire is easier to work with than the hexagonal type sold as chicken wire. The dimensions of the mesh are important for keeping rodents from the aviary. For this reason, it should ideally be 1.25 cm (½ in) square, but in view of the spiralling costs of both wire and timber in recent

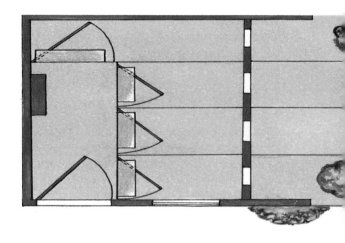

years, 2.5 cm x 1.25 cm (1 x ½ in) will be effective in excluding all but the smallest mice.

Ground plan of the aviary shown previously. A series of doors allows access to each of the four flight-and-shelter areas both from outside and from the service space.

Cost savings

Considerable savings on the cost of building an aviary can be made by purchasing the mesh at discount prices from one of the firms which advertise in bird-keeping magazines. Slightly damaged rolls can also be obtained on occasion, at even bigger reductions. Wood suitable for the framework is often available from demolition contractors; providing it has not been chemically treated in any way and is free from woodworm, this can represent a further saving.

Making the flight framework To protect the external framework from the elements, the lengths of timber should be treated initially with a safe wood preservative. After being given several coats over a period of a few days, it should be left to dry thoroughly until it is safe for the budgerigars. Subsequently, the timber can be made into the frames, which should be jointed. These joints can be fixed by either screws or nails, and then the panels of the flight can be

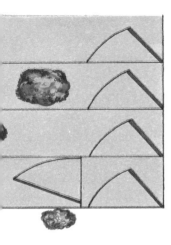

dangerous cut ends of wire will be out of reach of the budgerigars when the frames are assembled.

As each frame is completed, it is useful to number the sides, according to their final positions in the flight, so there should be no confusion when the structure is being erected. Irrespective of the floor covering, the flight, as well as the shelter, should be mounted on brickwork, extending for at least 30 cm (1 ft) below ground level, and 15 cm (6 in) above it. This will help to give the structure stability and prevent it from rotting, while also serving to deter

wired.

Wiring the panels Each panel in turn should be laid on flat ground and the wire cut so that ultimately it will cover the framework completely. It is useful to allow a slight overlap top and bottom when cutting the mesh. The inner surface of the flight must be covered completely, to protect the woodwork.

The assistance of another person is of great value in keeping the mesh taut and square on the frame. Netting staples are most convenient for attaching the aviary wire, and having tacked it in place at all the corners, the extra length allowed top and bottom can be bent over, on to the adjoining face of the wood. Here these potentially

With species that are inclined to gnaw, the wire mesh is stapled to the inside of the wooden framing of the aviary.

Attractive because of its low cost, hexagonal mesh has little rigidity of its own, which makes it best suited to indoor uses.

drilled for the bolts, can be placed in position on a further layer of wet cement. Finally, masonry nails can be driven through the woodwork into the bricks below, to make the finished structure as firm as possible. Neighboring frames should be held together with bolts and washers, and if these are oiled regularly, dismantling the structure later will pose no problems.

SHELTERS

Budgerigars, although hardy birds, require dry, draft-free roosting quarters attached to their flight area. As an adjunct to a flight 270 cm (9 ft) in length and 90 cm (3 ft) wide, the shelter should be at least 90 cm (3 ft) square. If the budgerigars will be breeding in the aviary itself, then the framework as built for the flight panels can be adapted to form the shelter.

Doors should be built into the back of this structure and also the front, which will eventually link the shelter with the flight. The outer door must include a window which ideally should be removable. The budgerigars will enter the shelter only if it is well-lit. On a hot day, ventilation

rats and similar predators from burrowing into the aviary itself.

Bolts should therefore be set into the brickwork to anchor the frames to the base. Once the mortar has set firm around them, the frames, with corresponding holes can be improved by taking out the window, which must in any case be covered with aviary wire. This serves to prevent the birds from flying straight into the glass and perhaps

In this aviary the opening between flight and shelter has been expanded to include a window, which provides additional light to the shelter.

guttering into a water-butt. The first 90 cm (3 ft) unit of the flight should be covered on the roof and sides with translucent plastic, to give the budgerigars some protection when they are outside in bad weather.

Materials used for the shelter The sides of the shelter framework should be covered externally with

killing themselves as a result.

The roof of the shelter should be covered with roofing felt, and must slope away from the flight. Rainwater running off the roof can be directed via

marine plywood or tongued-and-grooved wood. Although expensive, both are effective draft preventers and are quite durable. The inner surface can be wired over, as with the flight itself, or lined with thinner plywood or oil-tempered hardboard. These surfaces can be painted with a light emulsion paint which will be safe for use with the budgerigars.

The main disadvantage of using a solid lining is that it could provide a refuge for mice in the aviary. Aviary mesh on its own, however, will not give any insulation, and dirt falling in the gap between the wire and the outside of the shelter will be difficult to remove, without taking the netting staples out at regular intervals.

As a compromise, therefore, a solid lining can be screwed onto the framework, and removed if the presence of rodents is suspected. Any exposed ends of hardboard must be covered with battening, 1.25 cm (½ in) thick, to deter the budgerigars from

gnawing holes, particularly in the corners. If they get behind it, apart from the risk of becoming trapped, hens will often fight viciously over this presumed nesting site.

Budgerigars benefit from perches made of natural branches: they provide something to chew, and the varying thickness exercises the feet.

Floor coverings The floor of the shelter itself should be made of concrete, laid to a minimum depth of 10 cm (4 in). Aviary netting should be set into this floor to deter rodents from burrowing in, and a layer of thick polyethyene above this will act as a damp-proofing layer. Newspaper makes an ideal covering for this floor, as it will collect the droppings and seed husks, and can be changed regularly.

The flight should also have a solid floor, preferably of concrete, or else paving slabs filled in with mortar. Grass floors invariably become fouled very easily, and the grass then dies off in patches, while drainage itself can be a problem. A solid base can be washed without difficulty and generally kept much cleaner. It should slope away from the shelter towards the front of the flight, where a drainage hole has been made. This however, must be small enough to prevent mice from entering the aviary.

Perches The budgerigars should be provided with natural perches, but from trees such as apple, sycamore or ash. Elder is also a popular wood, and the birds will derive much pleasure from nibbling off the bark. Such perches will need to be replaced at regular intervals—they should be obtained from trees on which no chemical sprays have been used. They should be washed before being put into the aviary, as a precaution in case they have been fouled by wild birds or animals. Some woods, notably laburnum, lilac and yew, should be avoided, because they are poisonous to the birds.

The perches should be fitted across the aviary, rather than lengthwise, because the budgerigars will fly predominantly up and down the aviary. Overhanging is not recommended, because the lower perches will soon be soiled by the birds' droppings. Wire loops around the perches, attached by netting staples to a nearby piece of framework, are the most convenient means of fixing the perches firmly in place.

Round dowel perches, used in many cages, are also suitable for use in

This perching arrangement facilitates the short-term holding of a large number of birds in a small space.

aviaries, but, as always, variety in the diameter and shape of the perching is preferable. For this reason many breeders have natural perches in the outside flight, with round and oval dowelling inside the shelter. Perch scrapers available at your local

the budgerigars to enter the shelter, while the platform gives them easy access. If there is no safety porch included in the aviary design, then this entrance hole can be used to prevent accidental escapes when the aviary is entered.

Provided temperatures do not drop too low, budgerigars may be kept throughout the year in simply built accommodations like this one.

petshop can be used to keep the dowelling relatively clean, while the perches in the flight will also benefit from being cleaned regularly.

Preventing escapes A small hole, 10 cm (4 in) square, with a platform outside, can be cut, high up, beside the inner door. The height will encourage

A sliding closure flap made of plywood and fixed in a runner, extending level with the outer entrance platform, is simply attached to a piece of wire passed though the aviary mesh and bent to form a hook. The flap can then be pulled over the entrance hole from outside the aviary, thus ensuring that all the budgerigars are safely confined in the flight when the outer door of the shelter is opened. The system is also useful for catching the birds, since they cannot keep disappearing in and out of

In this birdroom, breeding cages constructed entirely of wire mesh have been hung in tiers from the wall. The outside nest boxes are made of cardboard.

the shelter to thwart one's efforts.

A safety porch, as its name suggests, is an enclosed area around the outer door of an aviary. Once the porch is entered and the door closed securely behind, it is then safe to open the aviary door. If any budgerigars do slip out, they will remain in the safety porch and can easily be returned to the

aviary itself. The extra materials involved do, however, increase the cost of the finished aviary quite considerably, compared to the system outlined above.

BIRDROOMS

The extra space which a birdroom will provide can be very valuable. Part of one end can suffice as a shelter, giving an L-shaped design with the attached aviary. The remainder of the area is then available for breeding cages, seed storage, and even perhaps an indoor flight for young stock or for selling birds. The budgerigars can all be attended to from inside, and, if a light is included, this enables their needs to be met after dark during the winter months. Indeed, lighting and heating will be essential if the budgerigars are being bred at this time of the year.

Facing page: Several pairs of budgies may be housed in a unit of this type. Each enclosure has a tray for easy cleaning.

Feeding

In captivity, budgerigars are fed mainly on the seeds of various cereal grasses supplemented with greenfood, grit and cuttlefish bone. The seed is largely responsible for supplying the carbohydrates, fats and proteins, with each group having specific functions within the body. Carbohydrate is used primarily to meet the energy requirements of the bird, while fat is a reversible means of storing excess energy, apart from protecting the vital organs of the body. Protein, in the form of its component amino acid residues, is utilized particularly for growth and repair purposes and so is required by young budgerigars especially, as well as those which are molting or breeding. In the seeds commonly fed to budgerigars these major food components exist in the following proportions: Canary seed: 55% carbohydrate, 4% fat, 16% protein. Millet: 56% carbohydrate, 5% fat, 14% protein. Oats: 60% carbohydrate; 6% fat, 12% protein. The actual percentages do vary somewhat between various samples, however, depending on factors such as growing conditions and the length of storage time.

SEEDS USED IN BUDGERIGAR MIXTURES

Young budgerigars enjoying a seed mixture and bits of fruit. The floor is covered with ground corn cob.

Most mixtures are composed exclusively of millet and canary seed; oats are fed separately, after being soaked. There are in fact several varieties of millet, which is the round seed in the mixture. Panicum millet, often fed in the form of sprays, also can be purchased loose, and is relatively small and yellow in color. The larger, pearl-white variety *(Pennisetum typhoideum)* is also included in many blends, but red millet is not generally favored by breeders.

Canary seed, like millet, is grown in the world's warmer regions, such as Africa and parts of Australia. The most highly regarded seed today is known as 'Mazagan', named after the area in

Utensils of this design may be used to supply either water or a seed mixture.

Morocco where it is grown. This crop is still harvested by hand in parts of the region.

Cultvation of these seeds It is nevertheless possible to grow both canary seed and millets in temperate climates. A small amount of home-grown seed is advertised every year, but even if the amateur's crop does not ripen completely, the seed-heads will be very popular with the budgerigars. The seed should preferably be sown in the autumn so that by the following spring, the young plants will be

established and should grow rapidly in the warmer months ahead. In a sunny location, the seed will be ready for harvesting from late July in the northern hemisphere. The stems can be cut and fed as required, or the whole crop, harvested at once and dried upside down in bunches, may be stored. It is probably most convenient to feed the seed-heads whole, although their contents can be extracted with careful use of a rolling pin and board.

Above: *Planted in saucers, seeds usually fed dry (and other grasses as well) furnish greenfood if allowed to grow suitably.*

Purchasing seed The condition of the seed is critical, and under no circumstances should damp, dirty or musty seed be fed to the budgerigars. For any given sample of seed it is not possible to determine its food value without a series of expensive tests, but some indication of its worth can be gained by noting the number of grains out of a hundred which will germinate successfully. Seed which has to be dried artificially may be overheated, killing the germ within and lowering the food value.

Reliable suppliers of seed can be found in the columns of most bird-

Below: *Bird seed is best kept in metal containers with lids that allow ventilation.*

keeping magazines. Local petshops or feed stores will often supply seed in bulk at discount prices.

Seed is usually sold in paper sacks, but these can get damp and may attract rodents, so for storage it should be transferred to metal bins with lids. Condensation in plastic sacks can saturate the seed within, and mold may then develop. These cereal seeds remain fresh for well over a year after harvesting, but their vitamin content will decline gradually over a long period; so, depending on circumstances, no more than two months' supply should be purchased at any time.

Mixtures There is a wide range of prepared mixtures of seed available, while many breeders themselves also formulate a ration, using the various seeds. Others offer the seeds in separate containers, and allow the budgerigars to suit their own requirements. This latter method does, however, entail more work if the birds are being bred in cages, as there will be double the number of feeding utensils which need to be filled and cleaned regularly.

The cheaper mixtures usually contain a higher proportion of millets, but they should never account for more than 40% of the seeds. When the budgerigars are breeding, the amount of canary seed should be increased to at least 80% because of its high protein level. Young stock and molting birds need to be fed similarly, begin germinating, with enzymatic changes reducing the food constituents to simpler, more digestible substances. Soaked seed is therefore of particular value to breeding birds, youngsters and those which are recovering from illness. The process is very similar to that which occurs naturally when

and it is particularly beneficial to supplement their food intake with a tonic at this time. Using seeds from various countries will help to guard against any local deficiencies.

Millet spray is a nutritious treat for a budgie, whether a singly kept pet or a breeder.

Soaked seed Exposure to water causes the seed to

seed is broken down in the budgerigar's digestive system, before the components can be absorbed.

The required quantity of seed should be soaked in

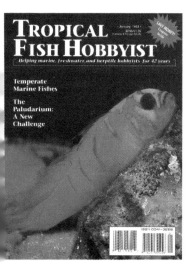

Since 1952, *Tropical Fish Hobbyist* has been the source of accurate, up-to-the-minute, and fascinating information on every facet of the aquarium hobby. Join the more than 50,000 devoted readers world-wide who wouldn't miss a single issue.

...From T.F.H., the world's largest publisher of bird books, a new bird magazine for birdkeepers all over the world...

CAGED BIRD HOBBYIST
IS FOR EVERYONE
WHO LOVES BIRDS.

CAGED BIRD HOBBYIST
IS PACKED WITH VALUABLE
INFORMATION SHOWING HOW
TO FEED, HOUSE, TRAIN AND CARE
FOR ALL TYPES OF BIRDS.

Subscribe right now so you don't miss a single copy!

SM-316

water overnight, for at least twelve hours, and then must be washed thoroughly in a sieve, under running water, before being fed to the budgerigars. Alternatively, at this stage the seed can be sprouted by leaving it on clean blotting paper in a warm environment for an additional three days, until shoots appear.

The danger with feeding all germinating seeds is that molds and bacteria will soon grow in a damp environment. If sprouted seed in particular smells unpleasant, then it should be discarded. After the budgerigars have had a reasonable opportunity to feed, any surplus, along with the container, should be removed. Millet sprays and oats are also often fed

Above: *Sprouted seeds are easy to prepare in a jar with a top that permits rinsing and ventilation.*

Below: *Green vegetables are nutritionally valuable, but budgies may not be inclined to eat them without coaxing.*

Attaching the cuttlefish bone to the cage wire helps to keep it from becoming soiled with droppings.

they are dissolved by the acid produced in the gizzard. A mixture of grits is recommended, however, so that there are also sufficient insoluble particles to grind up the food and prevent pieces from adhering together. Sea sand, mixed with limestone or oyster shell, is suitable for this purpose. Many packaged grits are available from pet stores, and it can also be purchased from most seed merchants.

Iodine blocks are of particular value for budgerigars, to prevent a possible deficiency of this vital mineral, used by the thyroid glands to produce a hormone which has widespread effects on the

in this way, but the amount of oats should be restricted because they can prove fattening.

Mineral intake These chemicals, required only in very small quantities in some cases, can prove vital both for breeding performance and good health. A deficiency of calcium, for example, is likely to lead to soft-shelled eggs, and so predisposes to egg-binding. Indeed, mineral shortages may also underlie may cases of death-in-the-shell. Seeds are generally deficient in minerals, and so supplementary sources have to be provided.

Soluble grits such as oyster shell contribute to the mineral intake, when

body's metabolism. Cuttlefish bone should always be available to budgerigars, and being an important source of calcium, larger quantities will be consumed during the breeding season. Such bones found on the beach, providing they are uncontaminated, can be cleaned, and then taken home and boiled thoroughly. After soaking in a bucket for a further week, during which time the water will need to be changed daily, the bones can then be dried off and

Above: *The tubular water font is widely used because it is hygienic and can be serviced easily from outside the cage or flight.*

Below: *Commercially prepared cuttlefish bone and mineral blocks make it easy to include trace elements in a budgerigar diet.*

used as required.

Vitamins Vitamins are complex organic molecules which play an integral part in many reactions taking place in the body. While deficiencies may have drastic effects, excesses in some cases can be equally harmful. For this reason, all tonics should be used in accordance with the manufacturer's directions. Supplementation may be necessary, because in many cases the vitamin content of seeds in relatively low.

Many helpful products, such as tonics and multivitamin preparations, are meant to be administered via the drinking water.

Vitamin A is not itself present in plants but a precursor, known as beta-carotene, is widely distributed in greenfood, and carrots are also a good source of this provitamin. This is then converted in the walls of the intestine and the liver to Vitamin A. Deficiency can cause weakness, poor hatchability and a high mortality in poultry.

Vitamin D_3 is also required by birds, and acts primarily to monitor and control the calcium stores in the body. It is produced naturally by the ultraviolet component of sunlight, which converts precursors present in the skin and feathers to the active form of the vitamin. Budgerigars breeding indoors, particularly during the winter, may be deficient in this vitamin.

Cod-liver oil is a valuable source of both these vitamins, and is often fed mixed with seed. It should be mixed in very thoroughly, at the rate of one teaspoonful to 454g (1 lb) of seed, daily as required. If the mixture is left for too long, the oil goes rancid, or if it is used in excess, Vitamin E deficiency may result; this is unlikely under normal circumstances, since a sufficient amount is present is seeds. There may also be a link between excess intake of cod-liver oil and french molt.

Budgerigars are often seen eating their droppings, probably because the birds may be deficient in some vitamins, such as riboflavin (Vitamin B_2). Cereals contain only small amounts, but since bacteria in the gut can produce this vitamin, the droppings often contain a higher level than the food itself. Folic acid derivatives, biotin and some other vitamins of the B group are also synthesized in this way, and overdosing with antibiotics may destroy these beneficial bacteria, leading to a vitamin deficiency.

Some breeders prefer to give a multi-vitamin preparation in the water, rather than cod-liver oil on the seed. The stated dosage should be given in plastic, not galvanized, drinkers. Other tonics are available in powder form and are given most effectively by being sprinkled on greenfood.

Greenfood Some form of greenfood should be provided daily during the breeding season, and the budgerigars will benefit from a constant supply throughout the year. It must be uncontaminated by any chemical sprays however, and so collecting sites such as roadside

Slipped through the cage wire, a piece of lettuce offered fresh daily is a simple way to supply greenfood.

It's prudent to wash chickweed and other greens thoroughly before placing them in the flight.

borders are best avoided. Chickweed is a particular favorite with most budgerigars, while young seeding grass, especially Meadow Grass *(Poa annua)* is also popular. During the winter months, spinach leaves can be offered, and carrots and apple will be enjoyed by some individuals. All food of this type must be washed thoroughly before being fed to the birds.

Aviary feeding

receptacles Metal seed hoppers are the most satisfactory means of feeding budgerigars in an aviary. A constant supply of clean seed is assured and wastage is negligible; the husks fall into a separate compartment below the feeding chamber. Open plastic pots attached by hooks should be used for soaked or sprouted seed and seed which has been treated with cod-liver oil. These feeders can be removed and washed daily. All food and water should be provided in the shelter, where the food will remain dry and prove less likely to attract rodents to the aviary.

Fresh water must always be available for the budgerigars. It is conveniently supplied in plastic drinkers, available in a range of sizes and designs. Water needs to be changed daily, and for large establishments, automatic drinking systems have been devised.

An open pot or a plastic drinker may be used to supply grit. Cuttlefish bone is easily attached to the aviary mesh by means of a special clip which can also be useful for holding greenfood.

Breeding

Budgerigars are very adaptable in their breeding habits and generally reproduce well when housed either as separate pairs in cages or together in an aviary. Disappointment is most likely, however, if only one pair is kept, because these gregarious parakeets seem to need the stimulus of other budgerigars in their close vicinity.

cleaner, the adult budgerigars kept in plastic boxes may show an increased tendency to pluck their chicks, as they have no wood to gnaw.

A suitable design The overall dimensions of the nestbox should be about 20 cm in length, 12.5 cm wide and 12.5 cm in height (8 x 5 x 5 in). The entrance hole, about 5 cm (2 in) in

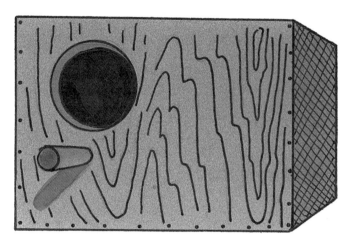

Nestboxes In the early days of budgerigar breeding, coconut husks were often used as nesting receptacles, but today plywood boxes are used almost exclusively. Modern technology led to the introduction of plastic boxes several years ago but these have not proved popular. Although the environment is perhaps

Nest boxes for budgerigars often follow this design: wider than tall, with the entrance hole to one side.

diameter, requires a short dowel perch just below it, to enable the parents to enter without difficulty. One end of the box normally has a sliding flap, which can be lifted up for inspection purposes. A piece of glass fitting between this and the interior of the box will eliminate the risk of eggs or chicks accidentally falling out of the nest when it is inspected. Furthermore, a gentle tap on the box will alert a hen to the imminent disturbance, and so she will have time to move aside, rather than to scramble out wildly, perhaps damaging her eggs and chicks.

Budgerigars do not use any nesting material and simpy require a concave surface on which they can lay their eggs and then brood the chicks. These wooden concaves can be purchased separately from nestboxes, and at least two per box will be needed. They must be changed at regular intervals, to keep the young chicks clean in the nest. The concaves need to fit tightly in the box, because otherwise young chicks can slip down between the concave and sides of the box and may die. They can sometimes be revived by warming them in cupped hands for a few minutes.

The concave on the floor of the nest box keeps chicks (and eggs) together in one spot.

Breeding cages When breeding for exhibition purposes, or to produce a specific color, the parentage of the budgerigars is vital, and so pairs must be housed separately. Suitable breeding cages can be purchased without difficulty, as individual units, or double and even treble series. Such cages, with removable partitions, are useful as stock cages for young birds, outside the breeding season, for example. It is also possible to obtain cage fronts separately, in a variety of sizes, and to construct cages to fit their dimensions.

A suitable design The cage should be as large as possible, bearing in mind that a pair may be housed therein for over seventeen weeks, if they have two rounds of chicks. A minimum length of 60 cm (2 ft) is advisable, to keep the birds in good condition. The cage should be made of thin plywood, rather than hardboard which is more likely to be chewed by the budgerigars, particularly if there are any small gaps to encourage them.

The plywood sides and roof are most conveniently painted before assembly, and then joined with small panel pins. A light emulsion paint will brighten the interior of the cage, and is safe to use, unlike lead-based paints which are liable to be toxic. A gap of at least 2.5 cm (1 in) must be allowed below the bottom of the cage front, so that a sliding tray lined with newspaper to catch the droppings and seed husks, can be inserted here. If a front with a height of 37.5 cm (15 in) is used, then the cage itself must be at least 40 cm (16 in) high.

The necessary holes for the nestbox and perch will have to be cut in one end, as it is preferable to attach the box outside the cage. Apart from giving more space inside, this will also make inspection and cleaning of the nest easier. Some cages have fronts which are designed to have a nestbox attached to them, rather than on the side of the cage, which means that it is possible to fit more cages of the same size into a given length.

Budgerigars seem to prefer cages located at least 30 cm (1 ft) off the ground. Using shelving, it is possible to stack breeding cages securely to a maximum height of three units. Under these circumstances the cages should be of a standard size and design, so the space available can be used to maximum advantage. Cages constructed in tiers are more difficult to maneuver than single cages, and if one pair is still breeding, then annual cleaning of a birdroom can be delayed.

Aviary breeding
Breeding budgerigars on the colony system in an aviary is an attractive way of keeping these parakeets, but it is not without its drawbacks. It may entail less work than breeding in cages, but problems arising from

new stock should be introduced during the whole of the breeding season, because this will upset the established pecking order, and fighting is then likely to occur. For the same reason, it is advisable to remove the mates of any birds which die during this time.

The nesting boxes should all be positioned at the same height, so that there is no competition to get possession of the top box. Allowing two boxes for each pair will enable the budgerigars to have an adequate choice.

After pairing, budgies are inclined to continue courtship atop the nest box they have chosen.

fighting are relatively common. One hen in a group often becomes a nuisance to the others, entering their nestboxes and causing eggs and chicks to be destroyed.

There are, however, several means of reducing the risk of such happenings. In the first place, the aviary must not be overcrowded, and the budgerigars should be kept only in pairs, with no odd birds, particularly hens, present in the colony. Furthermore, no

Pairing up There is no control over matings in the flight, and over a period of several years, the stock is likely to become closely related, so a proportion of new budgerigars should be introduced each year. If there is a specific pair which it is hoped will breed together, then they should be caught up and caged for two weeks before the nestboxes are introduced. This may encourage them to stay together, but budgerigars are fickle and so there is no guarantee that it will prove effective. Fertility is generally improved by allowing the birds to select their own mates.

Winter breeding

Budgerigars will often breed at all times of the year, when kept under artificial conditions. Exhibition breeders in the northern hemisphere may start pairing up their birds as early as Christmas, with the show season commencing the following July. This necessitates the use of both artificial heat and lighting to achieve the best results during these colder months.

Temperature Electrical tubular heaters are the only safe means of maintaining an even temperature in the birdroom, and it is possible to use these in conjunction with thermostats to keep costs to a minimum. There is some dispute over the correct setting, but the temperature of about 10°C (50°F) will be satisfactory. The size of the heater required obviously depends on the area which needs to be heated.

Humidity A reasonable degree of humidity is also necessary to ensure that the eggs hatch, and many breeders also have humidifiers connected into the electrical circuit. The humidity can be monitored easily by a hygrometer,

obtainable from hardware stores, and obviously a thermometer will also be required.

Light The budgerigars need sufficient light to feed their chicks adequately on a dark winter's night,

Installing the nest box outside the cage facilitates nest inspection. Hens often are so confiding that they will not leave the nest box.

requiring a total of twelve hours of light, including daylight. It is possible to purchase dimmers for the lights so that darkness falls gradually, rather than suddenly, perhaps stranding hens out of their nestboxes. A time-switch included in the lighting system allows adjustments to be made, as the days begin to lengthen in the spring.

Natural breeding season

For those without heating or lighting, it is usually safe to start breeding budgerigars from late March on in northern latitudes, once the risk of cold spells is virtually over. Nestboxes in an outside flight must be under cover, however, because they are liable to get flooded in a sudden summer downpour.

One element of courtship is mutual preening; here the hen is readily told by her darkened cere.

Budgerigars in breeding condition

Whatever their surroundings, the budgerigars must be in good condition before they will start to breed. The ceres of hen birds at this time will be deep brown, while cocks will be in tight feather, sing frequently and are often seen tapping their beaks on a perch. They start feeding their intended mates, and contract the pupils of the eyes, before mating takes place.

If the budgerigars are transferred to a breeding cage, then the entrance hole of the nestbox should be closed over for three days after the pair has been placed in the cage, in order to increase the chances of successful mating. The two perches, running across the cage from front to back, should have been fixed firmly in position beforehand, enabling the birds to mate without difficulty. Canning jars filled with seed and inverted on special plastic bases are the easiest means of feeding budgerigars in breeding cages. They need to be checked daily however, since occasionally the seed flow may become obstructed.

No pair should be allowed to rear more than two rounds of chicks in a year because it can prove a considerable drain on their stamina. In recent years there has been a trend towards offering high-protein rearing food to breeding budgerigars, in addition to soaked seed and greenfood. Such foods, if they are accepted, are of great value in rearing healthy chicks. For pairs reluctant to sample them, greenfood placed atop them can encourage the budgerigars to take this new addition to their diet.

Laying and the incubation period

Cuttlefish bone will be consumed in large quantities at this time, and, immediately prior to laying, the hen's droppings will appear larger and she may be slightly swollen around the vent. The white eggs are laid on alternate days as a rule, and although the average number in a clutch is about four, in excess of eight eggs is known. The date on which the first egg was laid should be noted and transferred to a record book where details about each pair are noted.

The incubation period is eighteen days, and the chicks hatch virtually naked, with their eyes closed. With a clutch of five eggs there is, therefore, an age difference of ten days between the oldest chick in the nest and the youngest. The hen sits alone, and is responsible for feeding the chicks herself for the first few days after hatching, on a secretion known as 'crop-milk', analogous to that produced by pigeons. In the case of the budgerigar, however, this high-protein food is produced in the hen's proventriculus, not the crop. The proportion of crop milk decreases as the chicks get older, being replaced by seed stored in the crop.

The rearing period With a nestful of chicks, the interior of the box soon gets very soiled. In some cases, the droppings stick to the claws and beaks of young chicks. This must be prevented at all costs, because it can lead to subsequent malformations. If excreta are caked on the feet, it must not be pulled off the claws, because the tips are likely to be damaged and start to bleed. The foot should be dipped in tepid water, until the dirt is softened, so that it can be removed safely. Changing the concave daily during this period should help to prevent the problems from arising.

Once the chicks are beginning to feather up, around the age of three weeks, the inside of their beaks should be inspected top and bottom for any food or excrement which has hardened in position. Unless such debris is removed, the beak is liable to grow abnormally. A blunt matchstick is a most effective tool for this purpose, enabling the dirt to be detached without too much difficulty.

The young budgerigars may leave the nest after four weeks, although five weeks is more usual. The hen will probably have started laying again by this time, and these eggs must be kept as clean as possible, to ensure hatchability, while some of the first round of youngsters are still in the nest. The chicks will be independent by the age of six weeks, and can then be moved to a separate accommodation, to check that they are eating independently. It is advisable to remove all first-round chicks from a breeding aviary, because they may interfere with the subsequent set of eggs.

Ringing and records No stud of budgerigars can progress without accurate pedigree records. Ringing, or banding, provides a practical means of identifying the birds correctly, as each has an individual number along with the year, as well as the breeder's code number

The difference made by the two-day hatching interval is apparent in this clutch of five chicks.

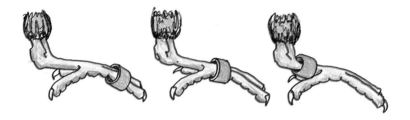

Here a closed ring is first slipped over the two forward toes; then the rear toes are pulled through with the aid of a matchstick or the like.

if official rings are used. These closed rings can be applied only when the chicks are in the nest, between the ages of five and ten days old. After this stage, the toes are too large to pass through the ring, and so it is best to ring the chick early.

There are two methods of applying a closed ring to a young budgerigar. In the first case, the ring is passed over the longest three toes to the base of the foot, and then the fourth toe can be pulled through with a ringing tool or matchstick. The ring should then move freely up and down this part of the leg, but not extend above the joint. Alternatively, it can be applied over the two front toes, and the remaining two are drawn through in sequence,

starting with the smaller toe. For some reason, in old birds the leg may swell under these rings, which then need to be removed immediately, or the whole foot may be lost. This is not easy however, because the aluminium of which the ring is made is tough, and veterinary help should be sought.

These closed rings are produced in a different color each year, so that it is possible to age a budgerigar in a flight by its ring color, without having to catch it. For simple identification purposes, celluloid split rings can be obtained in a wide range of single and dual colors. These can be applied at any age, because they merely slip over the leg. They can be used in conjunction with the aluminum rings, so that surplus budgerigars in the flight, for example, may be recognized at a glance.

BREEDING PROBLEMS:
No eggs Although most

pairs will go to nest without problems, every breeder does encounter difficulties with some birds on occasion. When a pair refuses to lay, it is likely that they are out of condition. If, after being returned to the flight for several weeks, no eggs are forthcoming, the birds should be separated and given new partners. Most pairs have eggs within a fortnight of being provided with a nestbox.

Infertile eggs The same technique can be effective with budgerigars which produce a round of infertile eggs. These are often referred to as 'clear', because after about the eighth day, a fertile egg when viewed in good light is seen to be opaque with the developing embryo inside. Clear eggs remain relatively transparent throughout, while those with discolored shells were probably fertile, but the embryo within failed to developed.

Dead-in-the-shell Dead-in-the-shell is relatively common, and may have several possible causes. Incorrect humidity, particularly at the end of the incubation period, is blamed by many breeders, while nutritional factors,

Barheads won't leave the nest until their feathers are nearly fully grown, that is, until they have some ability to fly.

especially mineral deficiencies, can also be implicated. Genetic defects may be responsible in other cases. Egg abnormalities are not unknown, and budgerigars have laid double-yolked eggs, which can, on rare occasions, hatch successfully to produce two chicks.

Egg-binding The management of the budgerigars is also undoubtedly responsible for some breeding problems. One study on egg-binding showed that the majority of eggs which could not be passed had abnormally thin shells. This suggests a deficiency of calcium, and certainly birds which are overbred seem more likely to succumb to egg-binding, as do young hens. These still require calcium for their own skeletal system, in addition to the extra requirement for breeding purposes. Hens therefore should not be used until they are at least a full year old.

The link between egg-binding and winter breeding can probably be traced in part to a Vitamin D_3 deficiency. In the summer, when ventilation in birdrooms is generally

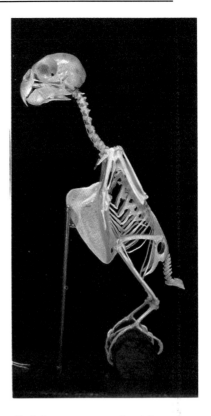

If dietary sources of calcium are insufficient while the hen's body is forming the egg, calcium will be withdrawn from the skeleton.

better with doors and windows open, the sun's ultra-violet rays, which cannot pass through glass, are more likely to reach the budgerigars. The vitamin thus produced is the controlling factor in mobilizing the body's calcium reserves. The lower temperatures of winter may also be involved, as muscular activity is likely to be depressed under such conditions. Breeding results at this time of year are, in fact, rarely as successful as those obtained during the summer, when the days are both longer and warmer.

Egg-eating Some pairs eat their eggs shortly after laying them, and this can be most frustrating. On occasion, only one member of the pair may be the culprit, and in a breeding aviary the pair whose eggs are destroyed may not be responsible. The problem can sometimes be overcome by placing an indestructible plastic canary egg in the nest. The only other solution is to remove the eggs as they are laid and foster them out to another pair. They can be collected by raising the concave a little on blocks, and cutting a small hole in the bottom, at the lowest point, so the egg falls through on to a soft bed of sawdust, out of reach of the birds.

The transferred eggs can be marked with a dot, using a felt-tipped pen, so it will be known if they hatch successfully. They should be added to a nest with eggs which were laid at about the same time. In fact, most pairs will readily accept other eggs, so if there are two nests, one with two eggs and another with eight, it does no harm to transfer three to the first. In these circumstances, it is particularly valuable to use a set of different color pens to dot each egg as it is laid, so the sequence of laying is known. No pair should be expected to rear more than six chicks at one time.

Feather plucking Feather plucking may start from a desire on the part of the adult budgerigars to get their early chicks out of the nest before commencing their second round, but this tendency soon becomes habitual. A nest of chicks may have their feathering devastated in this way in the course of just one morning. Although new feathers develop, plucked chicks are often more nervous than usual, and it would appear that this behavior could be inherited in some cases, so they are probably best kept as pets.

Fostering If either member of a pair dies while breeding, any eggs should be transferred to another pair. When a cock dies however, with chicks in the nest, many hens will rear these successfully by themselves. They should be watched closely, and left with a maximum of two chicks only, if possible, so they are not overburdened. Other pairs will readily adopt young from different nests, particularly when the chicks are under three weeks of age.

The youngsters of the fostering pair should be taken out of their nest and placed in a small box while the concave is changed. They can then be put back, along with the additional chicks, and the pair given some greenfood to distract

which does not have chicks at that stage to take a young budgerigar is likely to result in disappointment. Their prowess as foster-parents has helped breeders of other parrot-like birds in an emergency. Budgerigars have even hatched and reared Ring-necked Parrakeets (*Psittacula krameri*), which are twice their size!

Some breeders will not use birds which are over three years old for breeding, but in fact budgerigars can continue

A breeding pair with their two youngsters between them. Both chicks look like the Cinnamon Yellow hen.

them further. A check several hours later should reveal that all the chicks have been fed. Fostering as part of a group is usually without problems, but persuading a pair

reproducing until at least twice this age. Subsequently though, their breeding performance is likely to fall off, and fewer chicks may be produced as a result.

Genetics and Color Breeding

The potentially complex subject of genetics has a simple origin back in the nineteenth century, when an Austrian monk, Gregor Mendel, began to experiment by cross-pollinating pea plants. He noted the characteristics of the resulting seedlings, and from these, he established the first laws for the science of heredity, which is now known as genetics. Mendel's laws can be applied, in the case of the budgerigar, to predict the color characteristics of the offspring from any particular pairing.

The anatomy of genetics

The term 'genetics' was coined from the genes, which determine the whole appearance of the organism, including its color. The genes are located on chromosomes, which occur in pairs and are present in the nucleus of every living cell in the body. The number of such pairs varies according to the species concerned, and in the case of the budgerigar, there are fourteen. This can be determined by a technique referred to as karyotyping, which separates the chromosomes so that they can be viewed and counted under a microscope.

Blue-series budgerigars are the result of a genetic mutation that inhibits the formation of a yellow pigment in the course of feather growth.

MAUVE	OLIVE YELLOW	DARK GREEN
OPALINE DARK GREEN	OPALINE SKY BLUE	OPALINE GRAY
CINNAMON LIGHT GREEN	CINNAMON GRAY	CINNAMON COBALT

The members of one pair of the chromosomes of a hen bird are always of a different length, and these are the sex chromosomes, largely responsible for determining the sex of the individual. They're represented as XY, with Y being the shorter member of the pair, while those of the cock are of the same length, and referred to as XX. The remainder of the chromosomes are known as autosomes.

Mutations A mutation is said to occur following a change in one or more of

Autosomal Recessive: Light Green × Skyblue.

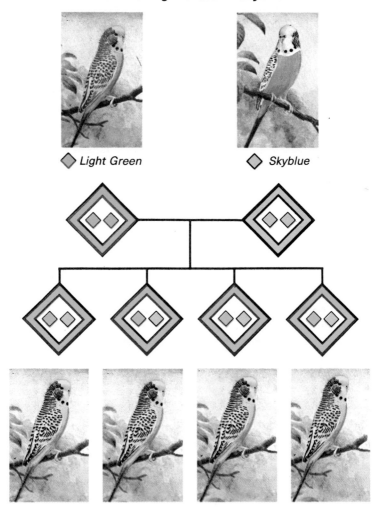

◇ Light Green   ◇ Skyblue

Light Green × Skyblue —→ 100% Light Green /Skyblue. This pairing is equivalent to Pairing 1 in the text, Light Green × Danish Pied. The genetic figures here and on the following pages employ squares, circles, and diamonds to show what offspring may be expected from a parental pair. Squares represent X chromosomes and thus also male animals, while circles represent the Y chromosome and female animals. Diamonds represent autosomes and therefore animals of either sex; in such contexts the sex of the animals is immaterial. The color of the border indicates the phenotype, while the inner colors represent the genotype by showing which factors are present on the pertinent chromosome pair.

the genes. Such mutations may prove lethal, and for this reason Crested budgerigars are not paired with each other if possible, because their crested chicks are most unlikely to survive; instead they are mated with non-creasted stock. Indeed, the vast majority of mutations are rarely beneficial to the species itself. Lutino budgerigars, for example, would be more conspicuous to predators, and their red eyes could prove an additional handicap in the bright sunlight of Australia. The chances of such a mutation surviving in its native, hostile enviornment are very remote, but under controlled conditions in aviaries, its numbers can be increased over a period of time, and used with other mutations to produce new color forms. The various budgerigar mutations fall into four basic categories: .

1. Autosomal Recessive

The majority of mutations are recessive; in the case of a Danish Pied budgerigar paired to the natural Light Green, no Danish Pied chicks will be bred in the first generation. All these youngsters nevertheless carry the mutated gene, and although they appear to be normals, their genetic make-up (or genotype) differs from their actual phenotypic appearance. Such budgerigars are often said to be split, indicated by an oblique line (/) for the color concerned. There are five possible pairings: 1. Light Green x Danish

Autosomal Recessive, Pairing 2:
Light Green /Danish Pied × Danish Pied

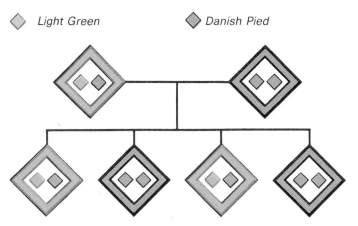

◇ *Light Green*　　◈ *Danish Pied*

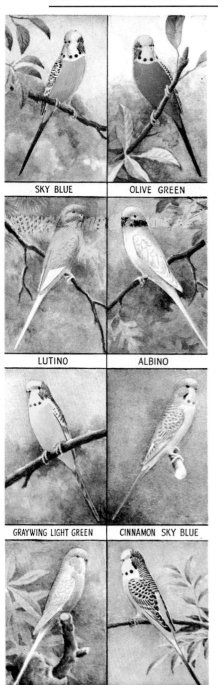

SKY BLUE

OLIVE GREEN

LUTINO

ALBINO

GRAYWING LIGHT GREEN

CINNAMON SKY BLUE

WHITEWING MAUVE

YELLOW FACE SKY BLUE

Pied → 100% Light Green /Danish Pied.

2. Light Green /Danish Pied × Danish Pied → 50% Danish Pied & 50% Light Green /Danish Pied.

3. Danish Pied x Danish Pied → 100% Danish Pied.

4. Light Green /Danish Pied x Light Green → 50% Light Green /Danish Pied & 50% Light Green.

5. Light Green /Danish Pied x Light Green /Danish Pied → 50% Light Green /Danish Pied & 25% Light Green & 25% Danish Pied. The actual proportion of Danish Pied chicks in any nest will vary, depending obviously on the parents,

as well as on chance, as all figures quoted in tables for pairings are based on the results obtained from a large number of nests and will not apply necessarily in individual cases. If Danish Pied chicks occur in the nest of a Light Green whose ancestry is uncertain, then the Light Green must be split for Danish Pied. Exhibition breeders often use Light Greens to improve the size and type of other varieties.

2. Sex-linked Recessive
Sex-linked recessive mutations are similar to the autosomal recessive type discussed above, but the genes affected occur

Autosomal Recessive, Pairing 5:
Light Green /Danish Pied × Light Green /Danish Pied

◇ Light Green ◆ Danish Pied

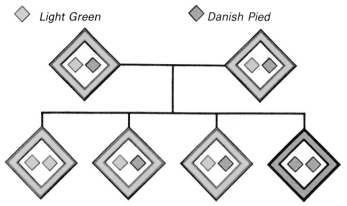

only on the pair of sex chromosomes, not the autosomes. Although a cock Lutino budgerigar can be considered genetically as a simple recessive, the hen, as already mentioned, has one sex chromosome shorter than the other. This means that such hens can be only Lutino or Light Green, never split for Lutino, and their phenotype must correspond to the genotype. There is no matching portion on the shorter Y chromosome for another gene to exert a masking effect on a recessive gene located on the corresponding part of the X chromosome. There are five possible pairings: 1. Light Green cock x Lutino hen → 50% Light Green /Lutino cocks & 50% Light Green hens. 2. Lutino cock x Light Green hen → 50% Light

Sex-linked Recessive, Pairing 1:
Light Green cock × Lutino hen

▪ Light Green ▫ Lutino

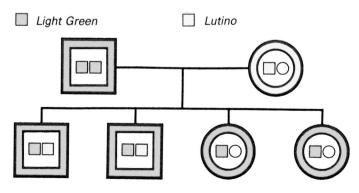

FALLOW LIGHT GREEN | WHITE or LIGHT SUFFUSION BLUE | DK.YELL OPALINE BROWNWING

Green /Lutino cocks &
50% Lutino hens.
3. Lutino cock x Lutino
hen ⟶ 100% Lutino cocks
and hens.
4. Light Green /Lutino cock
x Light Green hen ⟶ 25%
Light Green cocks, 25%
Light Green /Lutino cocks,
25% Light Green hens &
25% Lutino hens.
5. Light Green /Lutino cock
x Lutino hen ⟶ 25% Light
Green /Lutino cocks, 25%
Lutino cocks, 25% Light
Green hens & 25% Lutino
hens.

An autosomal form of both
Lutino and Albino
budgerigars was bred, but
the strain disappeared, so
only sex-linked types are
likely to be encountered at
present.

3. Dominant
Such mutations are
generally rare, being
known as dominant
because any budgerigars
of this type will, when
paired to Light Greens,
yield a proportion of
similarly colored offspring

Sex-linked Recessive, Pairing 5:
Light Green /Lutino cock × Lutino hen

☐ *Light Green*   ☐ *Lutino*

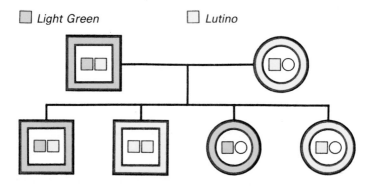

in the first generation, in contrast to the recessive mutations above. Considering the Dominant Pied mutation, it can be present in the genotype as a single or double factor, although separation between the two forms is possible only by trial pairings. If any Light Green chicks occur in the nest from Light Green and Dominant Pied parents, then the pied must be a single-factor bird. As this mutation is dominant, then it cannot be masked by Light Green, and so no Light Green /Dominant Pied budgerigars can be bred. The various possible pairings are:

1. Dominant Pied (double factor) x Light Green → 100% Dominant Pied (single factor).

2. Dominant Pied (single factor) x Light Green → 50% Dominant Pied (single factor) & 50% Light Green.

3. Dominant Pied (double factor) x Dominant Pied (double factor) → 100% Dominant Pied (double factor).

4. Dominant Pied (single factor) x Dominant Pied (single factor) → 50% Dominant Pied (single factor), 25% Dominant Pied (double factor) & 25% Light Green.

LIGHT YELLOW · LIGHT GREEN

VIOLET · GRAY GREEN

OPALINE BROWNWING COBALT · BLACK-EYED LUTINO

YELLOW-WING OLIVE GREEN · WHITEWING VIOLET

The band of white across the lower breast is characteristic of Dominant Pied varieties.

5. Dominant Pied (single factor) x Dominant Pied (double factor) → 50% Dominant Pied (single factor) & 50% Dominant Pied (double factor)

4. Incomplete Dominance

This method of inheritance applies to the dark factor, rather than to a specific color, and it can be present in single or double quantities. It is not confined to a specific color:

No dark factor: Light Green — Sky Blue. One dark factor: Dark Green — Cobalt. Two dark factors: Olive — Mauve.

Using the Green series as an example, the following pairings can be made:

1. Olive (double factor) x Light Green → 100% Dark Green.
2. Olive (double factor) x Dark Green (single factor) → 50% Olive (double factor) & 50% Dark Green (single factor).
3. Olive (double factor) x Olive (double factor) → 100% Olive (double factor).
4. Dark Green (single factor) x Light Green →

Dominant, Pairing 4:
Dominant Pied (S. F.) × Dominant Pied (S. F.)

◆ Dominant Pied   ◇ Light Green

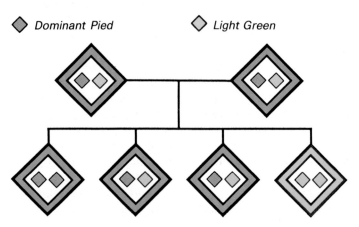

50% Dark Green (single factor) & 50% Light Green.

5. Dark Green (single factor) x Dark Green (single factor) → 50% Dark Green (single factor), 25% Olive (double factor) & 25% Light Green.

The same results can be expected using the corresponding blue forms.

part of the feather; and melanin, mainly responsible for black coloration, in the innermost portion. There is no blue pigment, but separating the yellow and black pigments is an area able to reflect light of a certain wavelength, creating an impression of blue.

Incomplete Dominance, Pairing 2: Dark Green × Olive

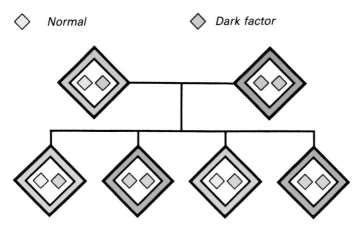

◇ Normal   ◈ Dark factor

How the different colors occur

The wild budgerigar is light green in color with black and yellow markings on its head, back and wings. The tail is tipped with blue, and the cheek patches are violet. This coloration results in part from color pigments, and also from the actual feather structure itself. The pigments fall into two classes: a yellow form located in the superficial

Mutations resulting from absence of pigments

Color mutations show changes in these pigments or in feather structure. The absence of yellow will result in a Blue budgerigar. Areas which are normally yellow will appear white, but as melanin is unaffected, the black markings are retained. A partial absence of melanin is seen in a Light Yellow budgerigar, which still

The pied factor, operating here in blue-series birds, brings about an absence of melanin pigment in certain areas of the plumage.

possesses cheek spots, and has dark eyes and legs. When melanin is lost completely, the Lutino mutation occurs. Like the Albino, which lacks both groups of pigment, it has red eyes and legs. A slight blue sheen is visible on Albino budgerigars, however, because the layer responsible for blue coloration remains intact, even when no pigment is present. Pieds generally show a localized loss of one or other of the pigments, and are, therefore, yellow and green, or white and blue.

Mutations resulting from structural changes in pigment or feathers

Cinnamon coloration results from a change in the shape of the melanin particles, so the budgerigar has brown rather than black markings. Darkening of colors, as seen in Olive budgerigars, does not occur because more melanin pigment is present, but is caused by an alteration in the feather structure itself. The layer responsible for blue coloration is smaller, so less light can be reflected, and more passes through to the melanin below, giving a darker appearance. This can apply to both green- and blue-series birds. Gray

Incomplete Dominance, Pairing 5:
Dark Green × Dark Green

◇ *Normal*   ◇ *Dark factor*

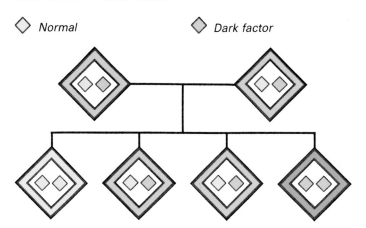

coloration results from alterations to this layer, as well as an increase in melanin production. Blues then become gray, while greens are darkened to gray-green.

Color inheritance in budgerigars
The following grouping can be made:

RECESSIVE MUTATIONS: Blues (all forms); Fallows (all forms); Yellows; Whites; Danish Pieds; Gray-wings; Clearwings.

SEX-LINKED RECESSIVE MUTATIONS: Opalines; Lutinos; Albinos; Cinnamons; Slates; Lacewings.

DOMINANT MUTATIONS: Australian Pieds; Violets; Grays; Clear-flights; Cresteds; Spangles.

It is, in fact, possible to have all three types of mutation present in one individual, such as an Opaline Crested Sky Blue. The dark factor can also be included to give an Opaline Crested Cobalt, if one dark factor only is present.

These birds barely suggest the many combinations of colors possible in budgerigars.

Budgerigars in the Home

Millions of budgerigars are kept worldwide as pets, and their numbers now surpass even those of the canary, making them the most popular companion bird. The budgerigar's pleasant chatter, tameness and ability to talk have assured its popularity in the home. Furthermore, suitable youngsters can be purchased at a modest price and are then relatively cheap to maintain, when compared with other pets such as dogs or cats. They are also ideal companions for those who, for one reason or another, cannot keep four-legged pets. Since a budgerigar can live considerably longer than ten years, it is important to choose a bird which will adjust well as a pet.

The budgerigar's vivacious behaviors and vocalizations make it a desirable pet for children.

Choosing a pet budgerigar A healthy young budgerigar about six weeks old will make a good pet. At this age the youngster will be independent of its parents, and, particularly if they have been handled in the nest, the majority are quite tame and may even perch confidently on a finger. Once they are over ten weeks old, even if they have been housed in a cage, budgerigars adapt less readily to separation from others of their kind. The largest selection of young birds is available

during the summer months, when many breeders have stock for sale, but they can usually be obtained in smaller numbers throughout the year.

Judging the age of a bird
Nestling budgerigars generally have blackish beaks, and the upper beak in a young bird may still show some darker markings. These disappear shortly after fledging however, and so are a useful means of judging the age of a youngster. Budgerigars, before their first molt at the age of twelve weeks on are often referred to as 'barheads', because the characteristic bars, which reach only to the level of the eyes on the head of an adult bird, extend right down to the cere in the young budgerigar. The cere itself is pinkish and prominent in a cock bird at this age, whereas that of a hen is both paler and flatter. In mature cocks, the color of the cere is blue, although it remains pinkish in the case of Red-eyed Fallows, Lutinos, Albinos and Recessive Pieds, while that of hens is brownish. Below the cere, on either side of the face, the throat spots of young budgerigars are

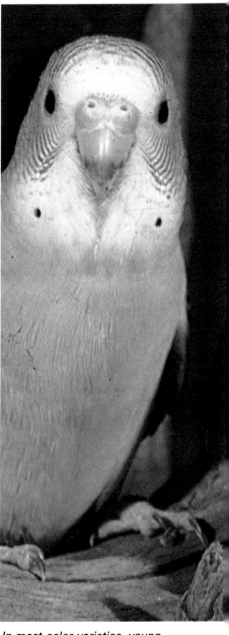

In most color varieties, young budgerigars have blackish beaks and barring from the crown of the head to the forehead.

65

reduced in size, and crescent-shaped rather than circular.

In varieties such as the Lutino, which lack melanin, the dark pigment, it is therefore not so easy to recognize a young bird, but the eyes provide a valuable clue. With the principal exception of Recessive Pieds, budgerigars only develop white irides when they are over twelve weeks old. This applies equally to red and black-eyed birds, but mature Recessive Pieds lack the irides. Once an un-ringed budgerigar has molted out for the first time it is virtually impossible to age it reliably.

Deciding on a cock or a hen Both sexes make delightful and entertaining pets; hens are more destructive, and do lay eggs. If these are taken away as they are laid, more will follow. The habit can be broken by changing the bird's environment, or leaving her with several eggs until her broody period passes naturally. Excessive laying is not recommended, because of the strain it imposes on the body's reserves.

HOUSING AND TRAINING: Cages Open

wire cages are most popular with pet owners, rather than the box cages used for breeding budgerigars. In the past, such cages were constructed solely of metal and glass, but now plastic is being used more widely. Many of the modern designs rely on a plastic

Owning a budgerigar along with other household pets presents no problems in most cases.

base, either clear or colored, which can be separated from the top wire unit by means of the sliding sand tray, which usually fits on the floor of the cage, when the cage is being cleaned. Such models are very easy to keep clean, since the base can be washed thoroughly and there are no crevices where dirt can accumulate. Similar cages, the bars of which are coated with a rust-proofing non-toxic paint, should last the bird's lifetime.

The largest possible cage should be obtained, particularly if the budgerigar is not going to be let out into the room for exercise. It is possible to purchase a stand for most cages, which should always be placed out of drafts and direct sunlight. Even new cages should be washed before being used, as they can get rather dusty while being stored.

Perches The perches should be positioned to ensure that the budgerigar's tail does not constantly rub on the bars, and that they do not overhang. It is a good idea to provide some form of natural perching in the cage, because many pet budgerigars develop sores

After a budgie becomes accustomed to its owner, it will perch contentedly on a finger (above). It may then be taken out and put back into its cage without the need for further handling (below).

on their feet if they are kept on dowel perches of uniform diameter. Alternatively, some perches can be planed down, to give some variation in grip for the bird. The floor of the cage can be covered with sand-sheets rather than loose sand, which can be messy. If newspaper is used, colored sheets should be avoided in case the inks used in their production are poisonous. Hen budgerigars in particular may chew up either the paper or sandsheets lining their cage, which is quite normal behavior.

Taming and teaching to talk The young budgerigar should be given several days to settle into its new environment, and then taming can begin in earnest. The first step is to get the bird to sit on a finger with complete confidence. This is encouraged by placing the index finger parallel with the perch; the youngster will soon perch on the finger without difficulty. Then the hand, with the budgerigar hopefully remaining in position, may be withdrawn gradually from the cage. Once this stage has been reached, it is then possible to train the bird to perch on one's shoulder and return to its cage.

Teaching the budgerigar to talk can commence simultaneously with taming. It requires only the patience to repeat constantly a simple word or tune, until it is imitated and learned, and then the bird's vocabulary can gradually be expanded in a similar way. Budgerigars of both sexes can talk, although cock birds are generally preferred by many people.

Because some plants are poisonous, the owner must take care that plants can't be nibbled from the cage, as could happen here, or eaten while the budgie is at liberty in a room.

Hidden dangers in a room No budgerigar should be allowed out of its cage into a room without constant supervision. Doors, windows and chimney exits should be closed before the cage door is opened. The window should be covered with net curtains; otherwise the budgerigars will not see the glass and may attempt to fly through it, perhaps with fatal consequences. Some house plants, such as ivy, may prove poisonous if eaten, and should be removed beforehand. Other pets in the vicinity can prove a hazard; cats are an obvious danger, but budgerigars have been known to drown in fish tanks when at liberty in a room. It is not advisable to keep these birds, even caged, in a kitchen, because the fumes can be dangerous to their health.

Exhibiting

The intending exhibitor, and indeed everyone interested in these parakeets, should join their national budgerigar society. They are responsible for the exhibition side of the hobby, and each member is usually issued individually coded rings, which must be used on young stock entered in breeders' classes at shows. The society will have a standard for exhibition budgerigars, and a system of points for judging the particular varieties. These vary somewhat: color is the important feature of good Lutinos, whereas the mask and spots are considered to be of equal importance in Light Greens. There are sometimes considerable differences between aviary and exhibition budgerigars, so anyone who intends to show birds is advised to visit local shows and breeders in the area to gain an idea of the standard and to obtain suitable stock.

Membership in a local club will also be helpful, and assisting as a steward at shows will give further insight into successful exhibiting.

The desirable intensity of color is apparent in this Lutino, as is the tucked-in beak.

EXHIBITION MANAGEMENT

The most important requirement for any budgerigar being shown is that it must be in top condition; this means feather perfect, and with no defects such as missing claws. It is a waste of effort exhibiting a bird which does not meet this condition, as it will have absolutely no chance of taking the coveted red ticket for its class (according to British regulations). Training is also an important factor in successful exhibiting, because the budgerigar must be sufficiently steady to be judged, rather than trying frantically to hide under the water pot on the cage floor.

Carefully drawn depictions such as this one help the exhibitor to visualize the "ideal" budgerigar. Particularly important are the proportions of the body and the disposition of the colors.

Training Every exhibitor has a preferred method of training stock, and there are no short cuts to success. Training should begin while the chicks are still in the nest, with regular handling to gain their confidence. By the time they are weaned, the youngsters should be quite tame, and at this stage can be introduced to a show cage for short periods. Standard show cages are likely to be required.

It is difficult to estimate the potential of a barhead as a winning exhibit, but the most likely individuals, assessed by their pedigree Promising birds can be caught at intervals, placed in show cages for up to a day, and then returned to their aviary. This serves to reinforce their earlier training.

Show preparation
Serious preparation for a show must commence at least two weeks

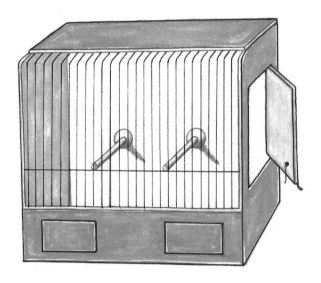

if necessary, should receive special attention. A pencil can be used as a judging stick to accustom them to movement close to the cage. Once they are about ten weeks old, the young budgerigars should be released into a larger flight cage to molt out, and their progress noted.

Uniform show cages allow judging to focus on the bird without being affected by how it is presented.

beforehand, and the probable entries kept initially in stock cages for assessment. It is essential now to avoid overcrowding, because the bird's condition is likely to suffer as a result. Feather damage can exclude a winning bird for some weeks; if a tail feather is broken, and the stub pulled out, it will take at least six weeks for it to regrow. Bent tail feathers can usually be steamed back into place using a kettle; great care should be taken to keep the budgerigar itself well away from the jet of steam.

Most budgerigars do not require washing before a show, but some can get muddy if they are kept on an earthen floor. The bird should be held as usual, with the head between the first two fingers on the left hand. Using the remaining fingers and thumb to restrain movement, the dirty areas can then be cleaned with water and a little shampoo. This must be kept out of the eyes, and rinsed out thoroughly afterwards, wetting the budgerigar as little as possible. Carrot must not be given before a show, because the juice can stain the bird's face, which will then need to be cleaned. If possible, the budgerigar should not be washed just before a show, to avoid unnecessarily upsetting it when it has to give of its best.

Training includes accustoming the birds to being housed in the show cage. In the exhibition itself, however, only one bird may be in each cage.

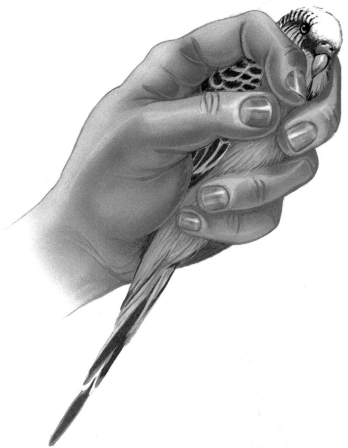

However, a daily tepid spray in the morning while the birds are indoors will help to maintain their condition. There are various preparations said to improve the natural 'bloom' of the plumage which can be added to the tepid water used for spraying. Many budgerigars have excess throat spots, and these must be reduced to give the even six required for

Holding a budgerigar in this way restrains the bird sufficiently while minimizing the likelihood of damage to the feathers.

exhibition purposes. The surplus feathers can either be tweaked out using a tweezers, or cut at their base with a pointed pair of scissors. This is not an easy process at first, and the help of an experienced fancier will be valuable in preventing mishaps. Cutting is preferable, because there should be no risk of bleeding, and the feather will not regrow until the remaining portion is molted naturally.

ENTERING SHOWS

Advanced notice of shows can be found in the various magazines covering budgerigars, and the first step for intending exhibitors is to obtain a copy of the schedule from the show secretary by enclosing a stamped, self-addressed envelope with the request.

Above: *Some shows provide trophies for winners, in addition to ribbons and rosettes.*

Below: *A Grey cock with a truly excessive number of throat spots. Choosing which feathers to remove will demand great care.*

The schedule should be read and completed with care, as a mistake at this stage could lead to disqualification later. Shows may be divided into sections for champion, intermediate, novice and beginner exhibitors. Each section is usually sub-divided into two, with any-age (adult) and breeders' classes. Only budgerigars which have been bred by the exhibitor can be entered in the latter classes. Older birds, and those bred by other people must be entered in any-age classes. After completion, the entry form is posted back to the secretary, with the necessary entry fees, and a stamp for return of

cage labels. These must be placed in the precise center of the front of the cage, below the bars.

The show The entries should be benched as early as possible, so they can settle down before judging starts. The cage floor must be covered with seed, but water is given only after judging, as a bird's appearance would be spoiled if it got wet beforehand. Exhibits may be judged without exhibitors being present, but subsequently most judges will help to advise a beginner about the standard of his entries. Judges, by virtue of their task, can rarely please everyone; but in fairness, it must be remembered that their decision can be made only on the budgerigars in front on them at that particular time.

After the show The budgerigars should be returned to stock cages after a show, to give them a chance to recover before being released into the aviaries, if they are not entered elsewhere for at least three weeks. Their cages will need to be cleaned thoroughly, and the labels removed in preparation for the next

This Skyblue breeder hen has won awards at several different shows.

show. They still require painting at intervals, because a poorly presented cage, though housing a good exhibit, will not impress a judge in the face of fierce competition. A matt white paint is used on the interior and bars, with a glossy black exterior.

Showing a good budgerigar too often will probably result in disappointment during the next breeding season. A show imposes a certain amount of stress on the birds, and so the number of outings must be restricted. These will be determined largely by the condition of the intended exhibit, and it is better from all points of view not to bench a bird unless it is in top condition. As hens can prove difficult to stage, preferring to search the floor of the cage for a nest, some breeders concentrate on maintaining a regular exhibition team composed mainly of cocks, while hens of the same standard are kept primarily for breeding purposes. The feasibility of this system depends to a great extent on the number of birds available.

Outside his aviaries, a Scottish breeder displays the trophies and rosettes he's won.

Health Problems

Keeping budgerigars healthy and in good condition is largely a question of careful management for they are generally hardy, robust birds. When problems do arise, however, an affected individual should be removed from the others immediately and transferred to a warm environment. The temperature should be maintained between 30-32°C (85-90°F), and a veterinarian's advice about possible treatment sought without delay. There are several hospital cages on the market today, equipped with thermostatically controlled heaters; these are also useful for reacclimatizing a bird which has recovered, before it is returned to its companions.

Antibiotics These drugs are highly effective in curing many ailments, but they need to be used with caution. In Britain, antibiotics for treatment purposes are available only on veterinary prescription, and the directions for their

Ill budgerigars often sit low on the perch with closed eyes and fluffed plumage. This bird is afflicted with French molt.

The large mass visible in the abdominal cavity is a tumor.

A SICK BUDGERIGAR

These parakeets are normally lively birds, and at first a sick individual will appear relatively quiet. This sign is particularly obvious to the experienced birdkeeper, who knows his stock. If the bird is neglected, its condition will deteriorate rapidly; the budgerigar then appears fluffed up, and often sleeps more than usual, its head resting on its back, and both feet gripping the perch (a healthy bird uses only one leg at a time to maintain its balance when resting). Depending on the illness, there may be other more specific signs; a

use must be followed explicitly, especially if elsewhere they are purchased off the shelf. Further infections, particularly by various fungi, are likely if antibiotic treatment is continued for too long, and other problems, such as infertility, may also occur. Indiscriminate use of an antibiotic on a group of birds is likely to lead to the development of resistant strains of bacteria, so that subsequent infections may not respond to this drug.

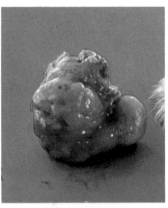

Budgerigars show a high incidence of tumors; the growth shown here was testicular.

stained vent indicates a digestive problem, for example. Budgerigars may look poorly when they are molting, and illness is often more common at this time.

Breathing disorders
There are many possible causes of wheezing and other breathing problems in budgerigars. One of the most common, especially in pet birds, is a deficiency of iodine in the diet, which in turn results in the swelling of the thyroid glands, which then press on the windpipe. In some cases, these glands may enlarge over tenfold, from a normal size of about 2 mm.

A range of bacteria, viruses and fungi can cause respiratory infections, which result in labored breathing, indicated by slow, irregular movements of the tail, and even pneumonia. A predisposing factor is often poor management, with the birds living in dirty, damp conditions. Antibiotic therapy may be effective in some cases, and the budgerigars' quarters should be cleaned thoroughly.

Pressure on the respiratory system, resulting from growths typically on the kidneys and reproductive organs, often causes breathing problems in an individual which otherwise appears healthy. There is no cure in this instance, and so the budgerigar will probably have to be destroyed painlessly, on a veterinarian's advice. Obesity, which commonly afflicts pet birds, may also contribute directly to breathing difficulties, as well as having other serious effects on the heart and circulatory system.

Breeding problems
Egg-binding, as explained earlier, is more likely to occur when the budgerigars are breeding during the colder months of the year. If unnoticed, the condition will soon

prove fatal, and so during the laying period the nest boxes should be inspected daily. An egg-bound hen initially appears fluffed up, and has difficulty in perching, often holding her legs further apart than normal. If left unattended, she will subsequently be be handled with the utmost care, because fatal peritonitis is very likely to develop if the egg breaks within her body. In some cases, it may be possible to feel the egg, very gently, just in front of the vent.

Warmth is of great value in assisting the expulsion

Egg binding often damages body tissue. In this instance the internal prolapse involved the small intestine and the oviduct.

found on the floor of the cage, in obvious distress.

When egg-binding is suspected, the hen should of retained eggs, and olive oil can be massaged carefully into the vent to give additional lubrication. Experienced fanciers can often remove such eggs successfully by hand, but, if no improvement results after the bird has been in a hospital cage for several hours, the novice should seek veterinary advice without further delay. An injection of calcium borogluconate can prove effective, while for a valuable budgerigar even surgery may be worth considering, although this is never without risk.

Once recovered, the hen should be kept indoors and reacclimatized before being released back into an aviary. She must not be used again for breeding for at least a year. On occasion, egg-binding is followed by prolapse, when part of the oviduct is visible as a pinkish mass protruding from the vent. It results from persistent straining of the abdominal muscles. The tissue should immediately be cleaned thoroughly with tepid water and smeared with a mild antiseptic ointment to reduce the risk of possible infection; it should then be pushed back gently, without delay. If the inflamed tissue subsequently re-emerges, then it may need to be held in place by a stitch inserted by a veterinarian.

Feather-plucking is a difficult problem to cure successfully, and although sprays are marketed as preventative, most appear to be ineffectual.

Feather plucking of nestlings by parents can be serious and difficult to correct.

Powdered bitter aloes applied particularly on the back at the base of the neck, avoiding the eyes, may deter some pairs from attacking their chicks in this way. It is also sometimes effective in deterring a known feather-plucking pair if applied to their youngsters as soon as they start feathering.

French molt remains a baffling phenomenon, but current research may soon reveal the main cause and probable predisposing factors. A viral involvement seems likely at present. In the meantime, there is no cure, but mild cases may

Above: *Persistent self-plucking in this case produced bleeding lesion.*

Below: *Stunted flight feathers are the most obvious manifestation of French molt.*

recover naturally as new feathers grow successfully. It is advisable to dispose of all affected birds, rather than retain them for breeding purposes, and to thoroughly disinfect the accommodation. The adults should be returned to a flight and given new partners in the following season.

Unlike the canary varieties that exhibit similar alterations in feather structure, the feather-duster budgerigar is short-lived.

Feather-dusters are also incurable. These are birds which develop well in the nest, but their feathers fail to stop growing normally, resulting in a grotesque specimen, which may not even be able to see because of its feathering.

These monsters, which have become more common in recent years, are probably afflicted with a hormone disorder. Even if their feathering is trimmed so they can feed well without difficulty, they rarely survive for more than a few months.

Digestive problems

Disorders of the digestive tract are one of the major causes of mortality in budgerigars. They often regurgitate seed naturally from their crops as part of the breeding behavior, and pet birds, especially cocks kept on their own, often attempt to feed a mirror or toy in their cages. In some cases, this can reach a stage where the budgerigar retains very little seed, and soon loses weight. It is rapidly fatal, and the only treatment is to change the environment of the bird, removing all toys from the cage.

This behavior should not be confused with the 'sour-crop syndrome', in which mucoid fluid, regurgitated along with seed, sticks to the feathers, staining them yellowish brown. In these cases, the budgerigar looks poorly and the droppings are abnormal, often predominantly whitish in color. The crop itself is often filled with gas, which can be removed by gently massaging the base of the neck. Potassium permanganate, sufficient to give the water a pinkish tinge only, often helps to assist in recovery, but in some cases, the disorder recurs at intervals. Seldom seen in hens with chicks, it can develop in other hens which are in good condition but not rearing a family. Protozoa have been isolated from such cases, and appropriate treatment with an anticoccidial drug offers the best chance of a cure.

Above: *Digestive disturbances sometimes result in regurgitated fluids soiling the plumage.*

Below: *An abrupt change in diet produced intestinal inflammation and diarrhea that caused the soiling visible here.*

Enteritis, meaning inflammation of the gut, is characterized by loose, green droppings which may be watery, or blood-stained in severe cases. Affected individuals should be isolated, as such infections can be transmitted via the droppings. The perches, feeding pots and other sites in the aviary should also be washed as a precaution against spreading infection. Dirty conditions, and the presence of mice which can transmit harmful bacteria to the budgerigars by contaminating seed, increase the risk of enteric infections.

Antibiotic powder given in the water, or treated seed containing a similar drug—obtainable from a veterinarian—is often effective in such cases. The situation is obviously more serious if a group of budgerigars are affected, and tests, including a post-mortem examination, may be recommended.

"Pasted vent" refers to dried fecal matter on the feathers surrounding the vent. In addition, here gout nodules disfigure the foot joints.

Constipation is, like diarrhea, not a disease in itself, but a symptom of several possible disorders. A budgerigar suffering from constipation passes fewer droppings than usual. The vent itself should be lubricated with olive oil, and greenfood, which has a laxative effect, should be fed regularly. An adequate supply of grit must be ensured. A little powdered charcoal, present in some grits, may reduce the risk of digestive disturbances.

Eye problems

Budgerigars of the red-eyed varieties are slightly more susceptible to eye problems than other types. In some cases, only one eye is affected, which often appears swollen, then becomes closed. An antibiotic ophthalmic ointment should resolve the problem quickly, providing the bird is restrained for a few minutes after application so it cannot immediately wipe the preparation off onto a perch. Drafts or a slight scratch can result directly in an eye ailment, but if both eyes are affected and the budgerigar appears fluffed up, with greenish diarrhea, it may well be a symptom of a much more serious generalized infection.

Growths There appears to be a slightly higher incidence of growths in pet budgerigars, as distinct from those living in aviaries. Reports suggest that up to 35% of all budgerigars will develop tumors, some of which, as in humans, are malignant, or cancerous, while others are benign. The reproductive organs, kidneys and fatty tissue are the most common sites.

The only treatment, where possible, is by surgery. Internal tumors are usually suggested by a loss of weight and condition. The cere color often becomes brownish in a cock bird with a tumor of the reproductive organs, while in the case of a hen it becomes pale. These color changes are not diagnostic however, as they merely reflect a loss of condition.

Injuries There is always a possibility of injury, but the design of the accommodation should help to minimize the risk. Loose ends of wire are particularly dangerous, and it is surprising how easily some budgerigars manage to become attached to such projections by their rings. There is a great danger of serious injury in such cases, unless the bird is restrained rapidly, and then extricated. If possible, the best solution is to cut off the offending piece of wire, freeing the budgerigar, and then gently remove it through the ring. Afterwards, the

ring should be moved carefully up and down the leg, to check for signs of injury.

Above: *Causes of a swollen eye may range from foreign-body irritation to orbital tumors—the latter is the case here.*

Below: *Brown hypertrophy of the cere resulting from a glandular disorder.*

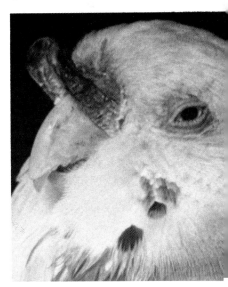

Cuts Minor cuts occur occasionally, often on the feet, and may first be detected by the appearance of blood on a perch. To decrease the risk of infection, the injury can be dabbed with a non-toxic antiseptic ointment. In most cases, bleeding will have stopped already, but if, for example, a nail has been torn or cut too short, the injury should be treated with a styptic pencil or dipped in a cold solution of potash alum, to stimulate the clotting process.

Fractures When a budgerigar has stunned itself, usually by flying into glass, there is really no treatment apart from keeping it as quiet as possible, in the hope that it will recover. Handling

Some fractures of the leg or foot may be treated in this manner, best accomplished by a veterinarian.

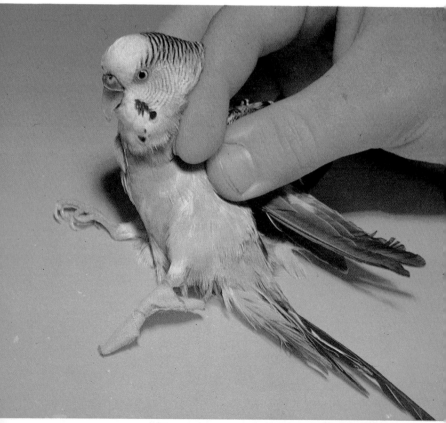

should be kept to a minimum. Suspected fractures require veterinary advice, and may have to be splinted. Successful recovery depends largely on the severity and position of the fracture. If a wing is broken, it usually hangs slightly lower than usual, while in the case of a fractured leg, the budgerigar will avoid using the limb. Some swelling can often be felt around the site of the fracture.

PARASITES: Mites There are two species of mite which are of particular concern to budgerigar breeders. The Red Mite (*Dermanyssus gallinae*) can be introduced to aviaries by wild birds in the vicinity. These minute parasites live in dark cracks in woodwork and similar sites, venturing out in darkness to feed on the budgerigar's blood. Birds which are breeding will be particularly at risk, because they spend most of the day and night in the nest box. Both chicks and adult birds are at risk, and anemia will develop in severe cases. Feather-plucking can result from the irritation caused by the feeding of these mites. Their numbers can increase very rapidly in

warm conditions, and they are capable of surviving in small numbers, without feeding, in cages or nest boxes from one breeding season to the next.

Regular spraying with a special aerosol which is safe for use on birds and available at most petshops will prevent these parasites from becoming

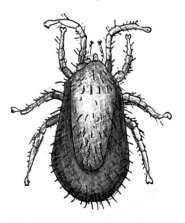

The Red Mite is a parasite that can be controlled quite readily.

established. They can be detected by covering a cage with a white cloth at night and then examining the inner side of this cover the next morning for small red specks, which are the engorged mites. Spraying as directed, coupled with washing the cage and nestbox as soon as possible, using a suitable preparation, will eliminate these pests.

An extreme case of scaly-face, infestation by a mite that burrows in the skin.

Scaly-face is caused by another mite, *Cnemidocoptes pilae,* which produces a series of coral-like encrustations, typically around the beak. In severe cases, it can spread to the legs and even to the body, and may lead to malformation of the beak.

These mites are probably transmitted directly from one budgerigar to another, particularly during the breeding season. Some individuals however, seem more resistant than others. Treatment is quite simple, and consists of applying a lotion or cream, obtainable from a pet store, to the encrustations. It is best to keep affected individuals in a cage for the duration of the treatment, and this also reduces the risk of spreading the mites to healthy birds. The cage should be washed with a disinfectant solution to kill any parasites surviving there.

Trimming beaks and claws The claws of some budgerigars, particularly pet birds, become overgrown, and there is then a risk that they may get entangled. It is relatively simple to trim the claws, preferably using a pair of claw clippers. In good light, the blood supply is visible as a thin red streak running down

For the health and comfort of the budgerigar, its overgrown beak and claws should have received attention long before this photo was taken.

each claw. The cut should be made a short distance from where this ends; otherwise bleeding will occur.

The beak can be cut in a similar manner, but it is not advisable to use scissors, as this tissue is much tougher than the claws. A check on the appropriate length should be made with other budgerigars. The top beak often needs cutting in pet budgerigars, which do not have access to branches for gnawing. Undershot beaks tend to develop particularly in the nest, perhaps because nest dirt is allowed to adhere to the soft tissue, distorting its growth, and so they too need to be trimmed regularly.

Suggested Reading

ENCYCLOPEDIA OF BUDGERIGARS by Georg A. Radtke (H-1027) In this most comprehensive of this well-known author's works on budgerigars, the initial chapters present an overview of budgerigars in the wild and in captivity, treat the various aspects of a complete budgerigar diet in detail, and then discuss breeding strategies and the prevention and treatment of disease. *Illustrated with 148 color and 44 black-and-white photos. Hard cover, 5½ × 8", 320 pp.*

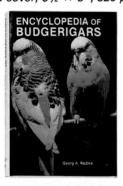

BUDGERIGAR HANDBOOK by Ernest H. Hart (H-901) offers complete coverage of every subject of importance to the budgerigar enthusiast. Included are discussions of modes of inheritance, basic breeding techniques, aviaries and equipment, feeding and management, shows and the Standard, matings and color expectations, and training the pet budgerigar. Color varieties are shown in photographs. *Illustrated with 104 color and 57 black-and-white photos. Hard cover, 5½ × 8", 251 pp.*

STARTING RIGHT WITH BUDGERIGARS by Risa Teitler (PS-793) was written to provide reliable, easy-to-understand information to new owners of budgerigars. The author is a noted bird trainer who draws on her special expertise in explaining just what to do when caring for, feeding, and handling a pet parakeet. *Illustrated with 67 color and 11 black-and-white photos. Hard cover, 8½ × 11", 80 pp.*

Index

Housing budgerigars in flights allows ample opportunity for exercise, which in turn conditions the birds for breeding.

Outside baths are attached to the cage at the open doorway.

A COMPLETE INTRODUCTION TO
BUDGERIGARS